REWARDS

Reading Excellence: Word Attack & Rate Development Strategies

Multisyllabic Word Reading Strategies

Anita L. Archer

Mary M. Gleason

Vicky Vachon

SOPRIS WEST EDUCATIONAL SERVICES
A CAMBIUM LEARNING COMPANY

BOSTON, MA • LONGMONT, CO

ISBN 13 Digit: 978-1-57035-272-0
ISBN 10 Digit: 1-57035-272-0

Printed in the United States of America

Published and Distributed by

Sopris West™
EDUCATIONAL SERVICES

A Cambium Learning Company

4093 Specialty Place • Longmont, CO 80504
(303) 651-2829 • www.sopriswest.com

24061/136/5-07

Contents

Letter to Students from the *REWARDS* Authors

Dear Students,

Welcome to the REWARDS program. This program will teach you how to read long words having two to eight parts. As you proceed through the grades, more and more of the words contain many parts. These longer words are particularly important because they often carry the meaning in content area textbooks.

In addition to learning strategies for reading long words, you will also be building your reading rate or fluency. As you know from your own experience, it is not only important to read words accurately but quickly. As you become a more fluent reader, you will be able to complete your reading assignments more quickly and will find recreational reading more enjoyable.

Hundreds of students have used this program in the past and found it to strengthen their reading skills. We hope that you experience the same gains and have ever increasing confidence in your reading.

May you reap all the REWARDS of this program.

Anita Archer
Mary Gleason
Vicky Vachon

Activity A: **Oral Activity—Blending Word Parts Into Words**

Activity B: **Vowel Combinations**

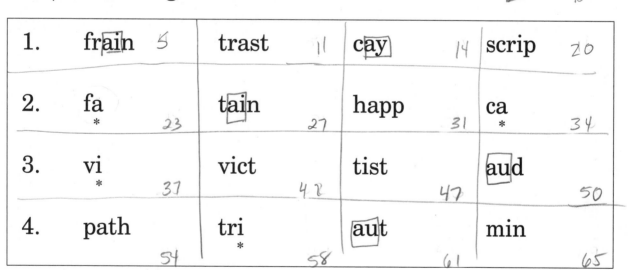

| ay (say) | ā | | ai (rain) | ā | | au (sauce) | ŏ |

Activity C: **Vowel Conversions**

☐ a   ā   i   ī

fingers
blend

Activity D: **Reading Parts of Real Words**

1.	frain 5	trast 11	cay 14	scrip 20
2.	fa * 23	tain 27	happ 31	ca * 34
3.	vi * 37	vict 42	tist 47	aud 50
4.	path 54	tri * 58	aut 61	min 65

Activity E: **Underlining Vowels in Words**

1.	waistband	fraud	plaything
2.	pigtail	vault	pathway
3.	waylay	launch	railway
4.	midway	blackmail	maintain
5.	applaud	layman	hairpin

sh !

Activity F: **Oral Activity—Correcting Close Approximations Using Context**

Activity G: **Prefixes and Suffixes**

discover	dis
mistaken	mis
abdomen	ab
advertise	ad

Activity H: **Circling Prefixes and Suffixes**

1.	addict	milkmaid	damp
2.	distract	ad-lib	disclaim
3.	admit	misfit	backspin
4.	mislay	misplay	distraught
5.	mast	banish	display
6.	misprint	distill	digit
7.	disband	abstract	mismatch

Activity I: **Vocabulary**

a. to not claim (Line 2, Activity H) _____

b. a person that does not fit into a group
(Line 3, Activity H) _____

c. a word or phrase that was not printed correctly
(Line 6, Activity H) _____

d. to not match (Line 7, Activity H) _____

Activity J: **Spelling Dictation**

1.	2.
3.	4.

Activity A: **Oral Activity—Blending Word Parts Into Words**

Activity B: **Vowel Combinations**

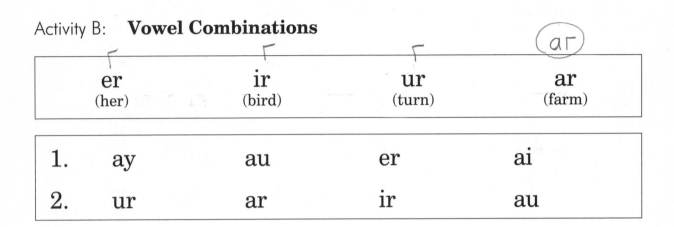

er	ir	ur	ar (circled)
er (her)	ir (bird)	ur (turn)	ar (farm)

1.	ay	au	er	ai
2.	ur	ar	ir	au

Activity C: **Vowel Conversions**

a	i	o

Activity D: **Reading Parts of Real Words**

1.	naut	tern	nay	bo *
2.	ston	auth	cur	turb
3.	fraid	irk	gar	darl
4.	sa *	pert	pi *	sail

Activity E: Underlining Vowels in Words

1.	garland	autocrat *	sterling
2.	birthday	verdict	fingernail
3.	goddaughter	whirlwind	modern
4.	pattern	curtail	surcharge
5.	auburn	vertigo *	astronaut *

Activity F: Oral Activity—Correcting Close Approximations Using Context

Activity G: Prefixes and Suffixes

insert	in
immediate	im
compare	com

1.	in	com	ab	mis	dis	in
2.	im	mis	ad	im	ab	com

Activity H: **Circling Prefixes and Suffixes**

1.	complain	indistinct	apron
2.	absurd	insist	discard
3.	disarm	ingrain	dinner
4.	command	imprint	inert
5.	administer	mishap	impact
6.	inlaid	darling	complaint
7.	impair	differ	disaster

Activity I: **Vocabulary**

a.	not clear or distinct (Line 1, Activity H) _____
b.	to take away arms (guns) (Line 3, Activity H) _____
c.	a print of a hand in the sand (Line 4, Activity H) _____
d.	laid into a design (Line 6, Activity H) _____

Activity J: **Spelling Dictation**

1.	2.
3.	4.

Activity A: **Oral Activity—Blending Word Parts Into Words**

Activity B: **Vowel Combinations**

	a - e (make)	o - e (hope)	i - e (side)	e - e (Pete)	u - e (use)
1.	er	ir	au	ai	a - e
2.	ar	u - e	ay	i - e	au
3.	e - e	ir	ai	o - e	u - e
4.	ur	ay	a - e	au	i - e

Activity C: **Vowel Conversions**

a	i	o	u

Activity D: **Reading Parts of Real Words**

1.	cue	ma *	plain	stile
2.	sud	mo *	haul	vate
3.	trode	aut	pede	larm
4.	murd	trac	mu *	bi *

Activity E: **Underlining Vowels in Words**

1.	turnstile	cauldron	austere
2.	shipmate	sunstroke	backbone
3.	holiday	autumn	umpire
4.	costume	stampede	subscribe
5.	obsolete	humanize	frustrate

Activity F: **Oral Activity—Correcting Close Approximations Using Context**

Activity G: **Prefixes and Suffixes**

belong	be	return	re
prevent	pre	protect	pro
depart	de	continue	con

1.	pro	be	pre	ad	dis	mis
2.	con	in	im	com	ab	de
3.	re	com	dis	con	pro	pre

Activity H: **Circling Prefixes and Suffixes**

1.	prepay	decode	readjust
2.	disgust	promote	mistake
3.	beside	conclude	pray
4.	defraud	combine	misplace
5.	intake	reconsider	confine
6.	reprint	impose	prescribe
7.	propose	discuss	advise

Activity I: **Vocabulary**

a. to pay before you get something (Line 1, Activity H)

_____

b. to figure out a coded message (Line 1, Activity H)

_____

c. to think about or consider something again
(Line 5, Activity H) _____

d. to print a picture again (Line 6, Activity H) _____

Activity J: **Spelling Dictation**

1.	2.
3.	4.

Activity A: **Oral Activity—Blending Word Parts Into Words**

Activity B: **Vowel Combinations**

oi (void)	ō ee	oy (boy)	ōr (torn)

1.	ay	oy	ai	er	ar	ir
2.	au	o - e	ur	i - e	oy	ai
3.	or	e - e	oi	u - e	oy	au

Activity C: **Vowel Conversions**

a	i	o	u

Activity D: **Reading Parts of Real Words**

1.	moil	straint	frant	mois
2.	sar	furn	mote	flo *
3.	tor	plete	cott	paup
4.	cate	stroy	saunt	mu *

Activity E: **Underlining Vowels in Words**

1.	turmoil	saunter	sportsman
2.	backporch	maximum	ordain
3.	murmur	loiter	boycott
4.	tabloid	vermin	tornado * *
5.	stockboy	popcorn	invoice

Activity F: **Oral Activity—Correcting Close Approximations Using Context**

Activity G: **Prefixes and Suffixes**

permit	per
uncover	un
above	a

1.	pro	a	pre	com	re	un
2.	in	ab	mis	con	pre	dis
3.	be	com	a	de	ad	per
4.	un	a	con	com	im	pre

Activity H: **Circling Prefixes and Suffixes**

1.	unchain	discomfort	prefix
2.	conduct	persist	confirm
3.	uncurl	reclaim	unfit
4.	alone	confide	misinform
5.	pertain	protrude	unsafe
6.	afraid	provide	disconfirm
7.	alert	across	demote

Activity I: **Vocabulary**

a. to remove from chains (Line 1, Activity H) _____

b. to remove curl from hair (Line 3, Activity H)

_____

c. to wrongly inform (Line 4, Activity H) _____

d. something that is not safe (Line 5, Activity H)

_____

Activity J: **Spelling Dictation**

1.	2.
3.	4.

Activity A: **Oral Activity—Blending Word Parts Into Words**

Activity B: **Vowel Combinations**

ee (deep)		oa (foam)		ou (loud)	
1. er	a - e	oi	oy	ee	o - e
2. u - e	ou	au	or	oa	oi
3. e - e	ir	ai	i - e	ur	or

Activity C: **Vowel Conversions**

a	i	o	u	e

Activity D: **Reading Parts of Real Words**

1.	gree	dain	des	fe *
2.	proach	snork	rupt	birth
3.	void	mount	spect	aust
4.	vide	teen	plaud	voy

Activity E: **Underlining Vowels in Words**

1.	freedom	filigree	voucher
2.	sweepstake	forlorn	canteen
3.	railroad	cloudburst	scapegoat
4.	spellbound	starboard	greenhouse
5.	outboard	roadside	textile

Activity F: **Oral Activity—Correcting Close Approximations Using Context**

Activity G: **Prefixes and Suffixes**

example	ex	
entail	en	

1.	per	con	dis	a	pre	de
2.	com	pro	en	ab	im	mis
3.	ex	con	un	com	a	pre

Activity H: **Circling Prefixes and Suffixes**

1.	exact	reproduce	beseech
2.	enclose	exceed	perturb
3.	expert	reconstruct	edit
4.	enlist	protest	engrave
5.	disagree	export	defame
6.	pretend	exclude	unpaid
7.	extreme	pester	imperfect

Activity I: **Vocabulary**

a. to build or construct again (Line 3, Activity H)

_____

b. to send goods to a port in another country
(Line 5, Activity H) _____

c. to take away someone's good name or fame
(Line 5, Activity H) _____

d. the opposite of include (Line 6, Activity H)

_____

Activity J: **Spelling Dictation**

1.	2.
3.	4.

Activity A: **Oral Activity—Blending Word Parts Into Words**

Activity B: **Vowel Combinations**

ow
(low)   (down)

1.	ou	ur	i - e	oy	ow	oa
2.	a - e	au	ai	ir	oi	ow
3.	ee	or	ar	oy	ow	u - e

Activity C: **Vowel Conversions**

a	i	o	u	e

Activity D: **Reading Parts of Real Words**

1.	dow	ster	ke *	spair
2.	feeb	slo *	croach	trow
3.	laud	flow	tope	aug
4.	coun	hale	fect	vent

Activity E: **Underlining Vowels in Words**

1.	pillow	chowder	shallow
2.	crossroad	flowerpot	sundown
3.	elbow	bowstring	fellowship
4.	outgrowth	trowel	nowadays
5.	electrode	windowpane	thirteenth

Activity F: **Oral Activity—Correcting Close Approximations Using Context**

Activity G: **Prefixes and Suffixes**

birds	s	frantic	ic
running	ing	regulate	ate
landed	ed	selfish	ish
		artist	ist
kindness	ness	realism	ism
useless	less	biggest	est

1.	com	a	pre	con	mis	de
2.	en	ex	per	dis	pro	be
3.	ness	ish	ist	ate	ism	ic
4.	less	ate	ish	est	ness	ist

Activity H: **Circling Prefixes and Suffixes**

1.	softness	astonish	extrinsic
2.	predominate	regardless	famish
3.	unselfish	ethnic	faddism
4.	alarmist	careless	loudest
5.	classic	abolish	degree
6.	hardness	exhaust	enthrone
7.	unhappiness	comprehend	hopeless

Activity I: **Vocabulary**

a.   not selfish (Line 3, Activity H) _____

b.   without care (Line 4, Activity H) _____

c.   to place on a throne (Line 6, Activity H) _____

d.   without hope (Line 7, Activity H) _____

Activity J: **Spelling Dictation**

| 1. | 2. |
| 3. | 4. |

Activity A: **Oral Activity—Blending Word Parts Into Words**

Activity B: **Vowel Combinations**

			OW			
			(low) (down)			
1.	oy	ow	ee	oa	ou	oi
2.	au	ur	ai	ay	i - e	ow
3.	a - e	ir	ar	oy	u - e	ur

Activity C: **Vowel Conversions**

i	e	u	a	o

Activity D: **Reading Parts of Real Words**

1.	stow	creet	cor	fir
2.	cloist	struc	vi *	low
3.	crow	floun	stay	lope
4.	sau *	cu	daunt	fide

Activity E: Underlining Vowels in Words

1.	snowflake	cowboy	flounder
2.	shallow	frown	showdown
3.	township	outgrow	showmanship
4.	boatload	rainbow	marshmallow
5.	downhill	stowaway	outstrip

Activity F: Oral Activity—Correcting Close Approximations Using Context

Activity G: Prefixes and Suffixes

careful	ful		farmer	er
tailor	or		final	al

1.	a	com	con	dis	pre	re
2.	im	ex	un	per	pro	a
3.	est	ic	ful	or	al	er
4.	ish	ism	less	ate	ness	ist

Page **20**   *REWARDS Student Book*

Activity H: **Circling Prefixes and Suffixes**

1.	abnormal	organism	tremor
2.	dishonor	ungrateful	proposal
3.	unfaithful	respectful	historical
4.	inventor	redeemer	untruthful
5.	personal	stiffest	programmer
6.	exaggerate	bemoan	regretful
7.	energetic	unfortunate	exotic

Activity I: **Vocabulary**

a. not normal (Line 1, Activity H) _____

b. full of respect (Line 3, Activity H) _____

c. a person who invents (Line 4, Activity H) _____

d. full of sorrow and regret (Line 6, Activity H) _____

Activity J: **Spelling Dictation**

1.	2.
3.	4.

Activity A: **Oral Activity—Blending Word Parts Into Words**

Activity B: **Vowel Combinations**

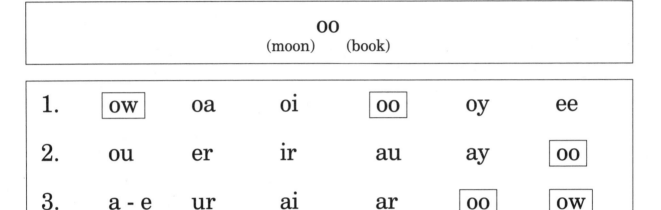

oo
(moon)   (book)

1.	ow	oa	oi	oo	oy	ee
2.	ou	er	ir	au	ay	oo
3.	a - e	ur	ai	ar	oo	ow

Activity C: **Vowel Conversions**

u	e	i	a	o

Activity D: **Reading Parts of Real Words**

1.	ploy	wood	lude	stound
2.	draul	perm	lo*	pool
3.	ti*	root	chowd	plore
4.	tron	plaint	tray	duce

Activity E: **Underlining Vowels in Words**

1.	boomerang	toadstool	loophole
2.	cartoon	shampoo	backwoodsman
3.	lampoon	hoodwink	roommate
4.	toothpick	footprint	tattoo
5.	whirlpool	macaroon	bridegroom

Activity F: **Oral Activity—Correcting Close Approximations Using Context**

Activity G: **Prefixes and Suffixes**

action	tion		attentive	tive
mission	sion		expensive	sive
million	ion			

1.	com	a	ad	com	pre	ex
2.	en	im	per	in	ab	mis
3.	ism	ist	ic	ion	tive	sion
4.	tion	ful	al	sive	or	ate

Activity H: **Circling Prefixes and Suffixes**

1.	unintentional	distasteful	deductive
2.	misconception	reestablish	billion
3.	preconception	opinion	conditional
4.	expansive	possession	exhaustive
5.	delightful	protection	external
6.	repulsive	percussion	provisional
7.	complication	adhesion	expressionless

Activity I: **Vocabulary**

a. done without intention (Line 1, Activity H)

_____

b. full of delight (Line 5, Activity H) _____

c. the act of protecting from harm (Line 5, Activity H)

_____

d. without expression (Line 7, Activity H) _____

Activity J: **Spelling Dictation**

1.	2.
3.	4.

Activity A: **Oral Activity—Blending Word Parts Into Words**

Activity B: **Vowel Combinations**

oo
(moon)   (book)

1.	ow	oa	ee	au	ur	ai
2.	oo	oi	ar	oy	or	oo
3.	u - e	au	i - e	e - e	er	ow

Activity C: **Vowel Conversions**

a	i	u	e	o

Activity D: **Reading Parts of Real Words**

1.	foot	vir	part	to *
2.	blow	ize	curd	ploit
3.	sault	press	hood	poon
4.	coll	vail	deem	ber

Activity E: **Underlining Vowels in Words**

1.	balloon	classroom	raccoon
2.	goose	scrapbook	woodchuck
3.	toothbrush	buffoon	uproot
4.	kangaroo	outlook	girlhood
5.	platoon	rooftop	stateroom

Activity F: **Oral Activity—Correcting Close Approximations Using Context**

Activity G: **Prefixes and Suffixes**

industry y		military ary	
safely ly		oddity ity	

1.	com	be	en	a	ab
2.	con	im	dis	per	pre
3.	er	ary	or	y	tive
4.	ion	ity	ly	sion	ary
5.	ic	sive	or	al	ful

Activity H: **Circling Prefixes and Suffixes**

1.	profoundly	absurdity	involuntary
2.	perfectionist	deliberate	collective
3.	liberalism	dictionary	contaminate
4.	incorporate	individuality	disability
5.	gladly	precautionary	personality
6.	independently	offensive	immortality
7.	incentive	confectionary	property

Activity I: **Vocabulary**

a. one who demands perfection (Line 2, Activity H)

_____

b. unique to individual person (Line 4, Activity H)

_____

c. to do something with gladness or joy
(Line 5, Activity H) _____

d. causing anger; giving offense (Line 6, Activity H)

_____

Activity J: **Spelling Dictation**

1.	2.
3.	4.

Activity A: **Oral Activity—Blending Word Parts Into Words**

Activity B: **Vowel Combinations**

ea
(meat)   (thread)

1.	oo	ow	ea	ou	oa	oi
2.	ai	au	ir	or	a - e	ee
3.	ea	oy	oo	ea	or	ay
4.	ow	o - e	ir	ar	ea	er

Activity C: **Vowel Conversions**

e	o	i	a	u

Activity D: **Reading Parts of Real Words**

1.	head	proof	trate	pow
2.	te *	bean	vant	mead
3.	oid	ped	vout	laun
4.	bard	bide	strain	glam

Lesson 10

Activity E: **Underlining Vowels in Words**

1.	peanut	coffeebean	beard
2.	yearling	steamboat	leather
3.	northeastern	steadfast	widespread
4.	farmstead	fountainhead	seashell
5.	headstrong	meadow	please

Activity F: **Oral Activity—Correcting Close Approximations Using Context**

Activity G: **Prefixes and Suffixes**

dorm**ant**	ant	disturb**ance**	ance
consist**ent**	ent	ess**ence**	ence
argu**ment**	ment		

1.	ab	con	a	com	en
2.	al	or	ly	sive	ance
3.	tive	ary	ence	ent	ant
4.	ity	ment	y	ion	est
5.	ful	ism	sion	ance	ant

Activity H: **Circling Prefixes and Suffixes**

1.	resentment	disinfectant	advertisement
2.	responsive	permanent	combatant
3.	excitement	disagreement	promotion
4.	compliance	informality	exuberant
5.	importance	insurance	continent
6.	rebellion	admittance	incoherence
7.	inconsistently	incidentally	experience

Activity I: **Vocabulary**

a.   an informal or relaxed act (Line 4, Activity H)

_____

b.   act of rebelling against authority; uprising
(Line 6, Activity H) _____

c.   admitting or allowing entry (Line 6, Activity H)

_____

d.   not acting consistently (Line 7, Activity H)

_____

Activity J: **Spelling Dictation**

1.	2.
3.	4.

Activity A: **Oral Activity—Blending Word Parts Into Words**

Activity B: **Vowel Combinations**

ea
(meat)   (thread)

1.	oo	ea	ow	ee	er	ai
2.	au	ay	e - e	oy	ea	ur
3.	oa	i - e	ir	ea	ar	oi
4.	ow	ur	ea	oo	oi	au

Activity C: **Vowel Conversions**

e	u	o	i	a

Activity D: **Reading Parts of Real Words**

1.	plor	hist	feath	cul
2.	read	gain	drift	bute
3.	pede	gart	ne *	stead
4.	ro *	story	caust	cen

Activity E: **Underlining Vowels in Words**

1.	earshot	bread	breakfast
2.	feather	letterhead	streamline
3.	readership	blockhead	jetstream
4.	seamstress	streambed	moonbeam
5.	meant	threadbare	headboard

Activity F: **Oral Activity—Correcting Close Approximations Using Context**

Activity G: **Prefixes and Suffixes**

nerv**ous**	ous	spe**cial**	cial
pre**cious**	cious	par**tial**	tial
cau**tious**	tious		

1.	im	a	com	con	en
2.	tive	ous	ion	or	y
3.	ary	tial	tious	ist	al
4.	ance	ment	ent	ly	ity
5.	ant	cial	cious	tion	sive

Activity H: **Circling Prefixes and Suffixes**

1.	tremendous	judicial	vicious
2.	spacious	social	substantial
3.	entertainment	marvelous	glacial
4.	compulsion	racial	initial
5.	pretentious	excessive	inconclusive
6.	continuous	gracious	indecision
7.	official	robbery	delicious

Activity I: **Vocabulary**

a. having much space (Line 2, Activity H)

_____

b. produced by ice or glaciers (Line 3, Activity H)

_____

c. full of grace and kindness (Line 6, Activity H)

_____

d. of or relating to a public office

(Line 7, Activity H) _____

Activity J: **Spelling Dictation**

1.	2.
3.	4.

Activity A: **Oral Activity—Blending Word Parts Into Words**

Activity B: **Vowel Combinations**

1.	oo	ea	oi	ow	er	ou
2.	oy	au	i - e	oa	ay	ir
3.	u - e	or	ou	ee	oo	ai
4.	ur	ar	ow	ea	au	o - e

Activity C: **Vowel Conversions**

a	i	e	u	o

Activity D: **Reading Parts of Real Words**

1.	thread	nore	ceal	ceed
2.	town	pun	pell	board
3.	cau	glor	na*	claim
4.	zoid	bount	gard	marv

Activity E: **Underlining Vowels in Words**

1.	waiter	daunt	monorail *
2.	prime-time	sidetrack	oilcloth
3.	torpedo * *	solitude	cockroach
4.	magnet	downstream	milkmaid
5.	marketplace	closet	bookcase

Activity F: **Oral Activity—Correcting Close Approximations Using Context**

Activity G: **Prefixes and Suffixes**

courage	age	disposable	able
picture	ture	reversible	ible
		cradle	le

1.	per	a	con	com	ex
2.	ous	able	ment	le	ent
3.	al	age	ture	cious	tial
4.	ion	ible	y	ance	or
5.	ity	ary	ence	ant	ment

Activity H: **Circling Prefixes and Suffixes**

1.	average	incombustible	inflexible
2.	conjecture	feeble	uncomfortable
3.	advisable	premature	mishandle
4.	predictable	adorable	inexhaustible
5.	nature	competition	incapable
6.	culinary	disadvantage	descriptive
7.	dependence	unobtrusive	unconventionality

Activity I: **Vocabulary**

a. cannot flex or be bent; stiff (Line 1, Activity H)

_____

b. easily foreseen or predicted (Line 4, Activity H)

_____

c. worthy of being adored, delightful (Line 4, Activity H)

_____

d. being unconventional or different (Line 7, Activity H)

_____

Activity J: **Spelling Dictation**

1.	2.
3.	4.

Activity A: **Vowel Combinations Review**

1.	oa	ay	oo	ee	a - e	er
2.	or	oy	ir	i - e	ar	ou
3.	au	oi	or	e - e	ur	ow

Activity B: **Vowel Conversions Review**

i	e	a	o	u

Activity C: **Prefixes and Suffixes Review**

1.	un	ab	dis	com	im
2.	be	con	pro	a	en
3.	age	able	le	cial	ent
4.	ence	al	sion	ant	ary
5.	ity	sive	ous	ment	ly

Activity D: **Strategy Instruction**

1.	propeller	construction
2.	infection	suddenness
3.	befuddle	instruction
4.	exterminate	commitment

Activity E: **Strategy Practice**

1.	expansion	unspeakable
2.	container	effective
3.	performance	consultant
4.	reunion	fraction
5.	furnish	inartistic

Activity F: **Spelling Dictation**

1.	2.
3.	4.

Activity G: **Sentence Reading**

1. The performance was very artistic.

2. Our new plane propeller is very effective.

3. The cruel words in the letter were unspeakable.

4. When construction is finished, we can furnish the house.

5. Everyone is sick because the infection spread.

6. Did you make a commitment to finish the work?

7. Can you exterminate the ants before they eat all the food?

8. The food consultant will help the people plan their dinner.

9. The man gave them instructions about how to furnish their house.

10. The container leaked; it was not effective for holding water.

11. The awful painting was completed by an inartistic person.

12. The new construction will result in expansion of the school.

Activity H: **Passage Preparation**

Part 1—Tell	
1. although	believed
2. justice	Europeans
3. Christian	language

Part 2—Strategy Practice	
1. escape	profitable
2. indenture indentured	colony colonies colonists
3. racism	superior
4. inferior	marketplace
5. Middle Passage	plantation

Activity I: **Passage Reading and Comprehension**

"Growth of Slavery"

9	Tidewater planters needed many workers to make their land profitable. At first, they tried to make Indians work the land. Or
21	they brought indentured servants from England. By the late
30	1600s, however, planters were buying large numbers of African
39	slaves. Although people in other colonies owned some slaves, most
49	slaves lived in the South. (#1)
54	Why did southern planters turn to African slave labor? The
64	English saw how slave labor earned profits for the Spanish
74	colonists. Planters believed that Africans were used to warm
83	climates. Then, too, it was hard for blacks to escape because their
95	skin color made it easy to find them. Unlike the Indians, Africans
107	did not know the forests of North America. (#2)
115	Planters preferred slaves to indentured servants because
122	buying a slave was a one-time expense. Indentured servants

132	could leave after they completed their years of service. But
142	planters owned and controlled their slaves as well as their slaves'
153	children forever. Colonists passed slave codes, or laws that
162	controlled the behavior of slaves and denied them basic rights.
172	Slaves were seen as property, not as human beings. (#3)
181	Most English colonists accepted slavery. They did not
189	question the justice of owning slaves because of racism. Racism is
200	the belief that one race is superior to another. White Europeans
211	believed that black Africans were inferior to them. They claimed
221	to be helping their slaves by teaching them Christian beliefs. A
232	few colonists, however, protested that slavery was unjust. (#4)
240	During the 1700s, the slave trade grew into a major
250	business. White slave traders built forts on the African coast.
260	They offered guns and other goods to African rulers who brought
271	slaves to the coast. Slaves were forced on board ships and packed
283	into small spaces below decks with hardly enough room to sit up.
295	Often, they were chained together two by two. Once or twice a
307	day, they were taken up on deck to eat and exercise. (#5)
318	Some Africans fought for their freedom during the trip.
327	Others refused to eat. But sailors pried open their mouths and
338	forced them to swallow food. Still others leaped overboard. They
348	chose to die rather than to live as slaves. Many died of diseases
361	that spread quickly in the hot, filthy air below deck. (#6)
371	The horrible trip from Africa to the Americas was called the
382	Middle Passage. When slave ships reached American ports,
390	captains sold their human cargo in the marketplace. Planters
399	inspected the slaves to find healthy, strong workers. On the
409	plantation, slaves had to adjust to a strange language and
419	culture—and to a life without freedom. (#7)
426	

From *The American Nation* by John Garraty. © 1994 by Prentice Hall. Used by permission.

A. ☐ **Total number of words read**

B. ☐ **Total number of underlined words (mistakes)**

C. ☐ **Total number of words read correctly**

Activity A: **Vowel Combinations Review**

1.	au	ee	a - e	ou	i - e	oo
2.	er	or	oa	oy	ay	ur
3.	ow	oi	ai	ir	ea	e - e

Activity B: **Vowel Conversions Review**

e	o	i	u	a

Activity C: **Prefixes and Suffixes Review**

1.	en	con	re	un	pre
2.	ab	ex	mis	de	a
3.	ness	er	ity	ism	ary
4.	ish	ture	tious	tion	ate
5.	al	tive	ent	ance	able

Activity D: **Strategy Instruction**

1.	commander	invention
2.	saintly	indifferent
3.	consolidate	adventure
4.	redecorate	projector

Activity E: **Strategy Practice**

1.	redundant	defensive
2.	proclaim	investment
3.	informative	concealment
4.	remission	fundamentally
5.	deliverance	determination

Activity F: **Word Reading Review**

1.	unspeakable	commitment
2.	effective	befuddle
3.	inartistic	exterminate
4.	fraction	propeller
5.	reunion	performance

Lesson 14

Activity G: **Spelling Dictation**

1.	2.
3.	4.

Activity H: **Sentence Reading**

1. Will you redecorate the house with new furnishings?
2. The book about engines was very informative.
3. Though Jane liked to paint, she was quite inartistic.
4. The commander who kept us fighting had great determination.
5. It would be a good investment to redecorate.
6. The defensive backs on the football team are explosive.
7. The invention will make the movie projector better.
8. Saying it over again is redundant.
9. The saintly commander helped the people find food.
10. What did the consultant proclaim he would accomplish?
11. Can you consolidate the cups into one container?
12. The colonists faced many dangerous adventures.

Activity I: **Passage Preparation**

Part 1—Tell		
1.	liquid	notice
2.	surface	reduced
3.	kilometers	process

Part 2—Strategy Practice		
1.	vaporization	evaporate evaporated
2.	evaporation	perspiration
3.	strenuous	particle particles
4.	ordinary	temperature
5.	conditions	altitudes

Activity J: **Passage Reading and Comprehension**

	"Liquid-Gas Phase Changes"
	Have you ever left a glass of water standing on the kitchen
12	counter overnight? If so, did you notice that the water level was
24	lower the next morning? Some of the liquid in the glass changed
36	phase and became a gas. The gas then escaped into the air. (#1)
48	The change of a substance from a liquid to a gas is called
61	vaporization. During this process, particles in a liquid absorb
70	enough heat energy to escape from the liquid phase. If
80	vaporization takes place at the surface of the liquid, the process is
92	called evaporation. So some of the water you left in the glass
104	overnight evaporated. (#2)
106	Evaporation is often thought of as a cooling process. Does
116	this sound strange to you? Think for a moment about perspiration

127	on the surface of your skin. As the water in perspiration
138	evaporates, it absorbs and carries away heat energy from your
148	body. In this way, your body is cooled. Can you explain why it is
162	important for you to sweat on a hot day or after you perform
175	strenuous exercise? (#3)
177	Vaporization does not occur only at the surface of a liquid. If
189	enough heat energy is supplied, particles inside the liquid can
199	change to a gas. These particles travel to the surface of the liquid
212	and then into the air. This process is called boiling. The
223	temperature at which a liquid boils is called its boiling point. The
235	boiling point of water under normal conditions at sea level is
246	100°C. The boiling point of table salt is 1413°C, and that of a
259	diamond is 4827°C! (#4)
262	The boiling point of a liquid is related to the pressure of the
275	air above it. Since the gas particles must escape from the surface
287	of the liquid, they need to have enough "push" to equal the
299	"push" of the air pressing down. So the lower the air pressure (the
312	less the "push" of the air pressing down), the more easily the
324	bubbles of gas can form within the liquid and then escape. Thus,
336	lowering the air pressure lowers the boiling point. (#5)
344	At high altitudes, air pressure is much lower, and so the
355	boiling point is reduced. If you could go many kilometers above
366	the Earth's surface, the pressure of the air would be so low that
379	you could boil water at ordinary room temperature! However, this
389	boiling water would be cool. You would not be able to cook
401	anything in this water. For it is the heat in boiling water that
414	cooks food, not simply the boiling process. (#6)
421	

From *Matter: Building Block of the Universe.* © 1994 by Prentice Hall.
Used by permission.

A. ☐ **Total number of words read**

B. ☐ **Total number of underlined words (mistakes)**

C. ☐ **Total number of words read correctly**

Activity A: **Vowel Combinations Review**

1.	ea	oi	oy	oa	ee	a - e
2.	oo	ur	ai	ow	i - e	o - e
3.	ow	oi	ai	ir	ea	e - e

Activity B: **Vowel Conversions Review**

a	e	i	o	u

Activity C: **Prefixes and Suffixes Review**

1.	in	dis	per	im	re
2.	con	un	en	de	com
3.	ful	sion	ly	ture	ant
4.	tial	ible	le	ence	y
5.	cial	al	ment	ary	ity

Activity D: **Strategy Instruction**

1.	consistent	amendment
2.	readdress	pavilion

Activity E: **Strategy Practice**

1.	intermission	dependent
2.	reflective	confederate
3.	amusement	intolerable
4.	potential	defender
5.	instructor	administrative
6.	discussion	unprofessional
7.	expectant	investigation

Activity F: **Word Reading Review**

1.	exterminate	effective
2.	consolidate	informative
3.	indifferent	adventure
4.	deliverance	investment
5.	concealment	fundamentally

Activity G: **Spelling Dictation**

1.	2.
3.	4.

Activity H: **Sentence Reading**

1. The instructor led the discussion.

2. The confederate army was the defender in the battle.

3. It was important to readdress the letters.

4. The amendment was passed after some discussion.

5. There was an odd expression on the instructor's face.

6. She is dependent on the consultant for help.

7. Lee had a commitment to the Confederate Army.

8. Four defenders on the defensive team were hurt.

9. There will be an investigation of the consultant's unprofessional acts.

10. Should we consolidate our investments?

11. At intermission, Trevor and Janis had an important discussion.

12. The performance was held in the Arts Pavilion.

Activity I: **Passage Preparation**

Part 1—Tell	
1. influence	bulimia
2. anorexia nervosa	periodically
3. psychological	nutrients

Part 2—Strategy Practice	
1. disorders	overeating
2. appearance	overexercise
3. extremely	essential
4. malnutrition	starvation
5. medication	abnormality
	abnormalities

Activity J: **Passage Reading and Comprehension**

> ### "What Are Eating Disorders?"
>
> 10   You can probably tell when your body needs food because
> 19   you feel hungry. Sometimes other factors might influence when
> 32   and how much you eat. For example, you might tend to eat more
> 42   when you are bored. Different people can have different eating
> 54   habits, but most people are able to control the way they eat.
> 63   However, some people have serious eating disorders that cause
> 73   them to lose control over their patterns of eating. Anorexia
> 82   nervosa, bulimia, and overeating are three such eating disorders. (#1)
> 92   Anorexia nervosa is a serious disorder that occurs when a
> 102 person avoids eating. Both boys and girls can suffer from
> 111 anorexia nervosa, but this disorder is more common among
> 113 teenage girls. (#2)
> 124 Typically, people in the early stages of anorexia begin to diet.
> 132 Some people diet to improve their appearance. Sometimes,
> 144 athletes go on strict diets to quickly reach or maintain a certain
> 154 weight for an athletic event. However, people with anorexia do
>   not stop dieting. They eat less and less. Soon they complain about

166	feeling full after eating only a bite or two of food. Often, anorexic
179	people overexercise to use up calories. Anorexics have an intense
189	fear of becoming fat, and continue to think of themselves as fat
201	even though they are extremely thin. (#3)
207	People with this eating disorder deprive their bodies of
216	essential nutrients. This disease leads to severe malnutrition and
225	can even cause death by starvation. (#4)
231	A doctor's treatment is needed to overcome anorexia. A
240	doctor may need to prescribe medication for malnutrition. In
249	addition, people with anorexia need psychological counseling to
257	deal with the causes of this eating disorder.
265	Bulimia is an eating disorder in which a person periodically
275	eats overly large amounts of food within a short period of time.
287	The person often vomits. Bulimia can cause serious health
296	problems, including severe weight loss, malnutrition, tooth decay,
304	and heart abnormalities. Medical and psychological treatment is
312	needed to help a person overcome this disorder. (#5)
320	You probably can think of some times when you ate too
331	much food. Perhaps you tried a dessert because it looked good
342	even though you were not hungry. Maybe you ate too much at a
355	large meal during special holidays. Most people overeat once in a
366	while.
367	For some people, however, overeating becomes a regular
375	practice. These people often eat when they are not hungry, and
386	they frequently eat without enjoying their food. People with this
396	eating disorder seem to lose control over the way they eat. (#6)
407	Overeating can cause a person to become overweight. In
416	addition, overeating can lead to malnutrition. While people with
425	this eating disorder eat large amounts of food, they do not always
437	eat food that provides them with the necessary nutrients. (#7)
446	

A.	[ ]	**Total number of words read**
B.	[ ]	**Total number of underlined words (mistakes)**
C.	[ ]	**Total number of words read correctly**

Activity A: **Vowel Combinations Review**

1.	a - e	ay	oy	oo	er	i - e
2.	ir	ow	o - e	au	or	oi
3.	oo	ea	ar	ow	ai	e - e

Activity B: **Vowel Conversions Review**

o	i	e	a	u

Activity C: **Prefixes and Suffixes Review**

1.	ab	de	mis	in	com
2.	con	ad	per	un	im
3.	ness	ence	y	ate	or
4.	ant	ment	able	age	ion
5.	ary	ist	le	est	tive

Activity D: **Strategy Instruction**

1. completeness	laminate
2. tentatively	decompression

Activity E: **Strategy Practice**

1. distrustful	unmanageable
2. missionary	intentional
3. completely	dissatisfaction
4. reduction	absorbent
5. astonishingly	discriminate
6. glamorously	immediately
7. apartment	enlightenment

Activity F: **Word Reading Review**

1. instructor	potential
2. amendment	intermission
3. informative	determination
4. intolerable	unprofessional
5. investigation	administrative

Activity G: **Spelling Dictation**

1.	2.
3.	4.

Activity H: **Sentence Reading**

1. The unmanageable work led to job dissatisfaction.

2. People who pray hope to gain enlightenment.

3. The instructor's corrections to the test were intentional.

4. We couldn't tell how she was feeling because her face was completely expressionless.

5. The astonishingly high heat in the desert is almost intolerable.

6. The students and the instructors came to the reunion.

7. Was there a reduction in the apartment's rent?

8. Apartment managers cannot discriminate against people.

9. At intermission, go immediately to the front desk.

10. The apartment was decorated very glamorously.

11. The athlete showed great determination during training.

12. How Mr. Hernandez completed his administrative tasks led to great satisfaction among the other teachers.

Activity I: **Passage Preparation**

Part 1—Tell

1.	Emerald Isle	Ireland
2.	famine	machinery
3.	European	ancestry
4.	Celts	Gaelic

Part 2—Strategy Practice

1.	surrounded	capital
2.	uniform	Protestant
3.	pasture pastureland	manufacture manufacturing
4.	emigrate	industry
5.	disaster	transportation
6.	equipment	official

Activity J: **Passage Reading and Comprehension**

"The Emerald Isle"

If you could fly over Ireland on a summer day, you would
12 see lush green meadows and tree-covered hills. Surrounded on
22 three sides by the Atlantic Ocean, Ireland's green color is so
33 striking that it was named the Emerald Isle. (#1)

41 **The Landscape**
43 At Ireland's center lies a wide, rolling plain dotted with low
54 hills. Forests and farmland cover this central lowland. Much of
64 the area is rich in peat, or wet ground with decaying plants that
77 can be used for fuel. Peat is dug from bogs, or swampy lands. (#2)
90 Along the Irish coast, the land rises in rocky highlands. In
101 some places, however, the central plain spreads all the way to the
113 sea. Dublin, Ireland's capital, is on an eastern stretch of the plain.

125 **The Climate**
127 Whether plain or highland, no part of Ireland is more than
138 70 miles from the sea. This nearness to the sea gives Ireland a
151 uniform climate. Like the United Kingdom, Ireland is warmed by
161 moist winds blowing over the North Atlantic Current. The mild

171	weather, along with frequent rain and mist, makes Ireland's
180	landscape green year-round. (#3)
184	**The Economy**
186	Ireland has few mineral resources. The country, however,
194	does have rich soil and pastureland.
200	The mild and rainy climate favors farming. In the mid-
210	1800s, Irish farmers grew potatoes as their main food crop. When
221	too much rain and a blight caused the potatoes to rot in the fields,
235	famine struck, bringing hardship to the Irish. This disaster forced
245	many Irish to emigrate to other countries, especially to the United
256	States. (#4)
257	Although farming is still important to Ireland, industry now
266	also contributes to economic development. The economy depends
274	on the manufacturing of machinery and transportation
281	equipment exported to the United Kingdom and the European
290	mainland. Ships bringing mineral and energy resources to
298	Ireland dock at the country's many ports, including Dublin and
308	Cork. (#5)
309	**The People**
311	Most of the Irish trace their ancestry to groups of people
322	who settled Ireland more than 7,000 years ago. The Celts and
333	British made the biggest impact. Their languages—Gaelic and
342	English—are Irelands' two official languages today. Most Irish,
351	however, speak English as their everyday language. (#6)
358	**Influences of the Past**
362	Stormy politics mark Ireland's history. From the 1100s to the
372	early 1900s, the British governed Ireland. Religion and
380	government controls mixed to cause disagreement. The Irish
388	people resisted British rule and demands that the Roman Catholic
398	country become Protestant. British officials seized land in Ireland
407	and gave it to English and Scottish Protestants. At one time the
419	British drove out Irish Catholics to make room for the new
430	settlers. (#7)
431	

A.	[ ]	**Total number of words read**
B.	[ ]	**Total number of underlined words (mistakes)**
C.	[ ]	**Total number of words read correctly**

Activity A: **Vowel Combinations Review**

1.	ay	a - e	au	oo	o - e	er
2.	ee	oi	ur	o - e	ai	ow
3.	ir	oy	ou	or	ea	u - e

Activity B: **Vowel Conversions Review**

| a | u | e | i | o |

Activity C: **Prefixes and Suffixes Review**

1.	a	pre	re	un	mis
2.	re	ab	con	com	per
3.	ic	ful	ly	ary	ate
4.	tion	ous	ist	ance	able
5.	al	sive	tial	age	ture

Activity D: **Strategy Practice**

1.	depression	exemption
2.	defendant	persistent
3.	destructive	communication
4.	commemorate	instrumentalist

Activity E: **Independent Strategy Practice**

1.	surrender	incorrectly
2.	expansion	government
3.	flattery	cultivate
4.	consistence	contentment
5.	unpredictable	inadmissible

Activity F: **Word Reading Review**

1.	completeness	reduction
2.	dependent	intermission
3.	discriminate	intentional
4.	tentatively	unmanageable
5.	investigation	dissatisfaction

Lesson 17

Activity G: **Spelling Dictation**

1.	2.
3.	4.

Activity H: **Sentence Reading**

1. Clear communication is important in relationships.

2. The Confederate Army had to surrender to the Union Army.

3. Most people cultivate their gardens in the spring.

4. The government commemorated the man's life with a special stamp.

5. Her actions were unpredictable, not consistent.

6. The investigation will focus on the main defendant.

7. The worker incorrectly connected the cables causing a power outage.

8. The government helped the people after the destructive earthquake.

9. The defendant was not given an exemption from paying the fine.

10. Jared no longer suffered from depression; he felt contentment.

11. Marty is an instrumentalist not a singer.

12. Maria showed great potential during her dance performance.

Activity I: **Passage Preparation**

Part 1—Tell	
1. circuits	chemists
2. pancreas	diabetes
3. bacteria	medicines

Part 2—Strategy Practice	
1. laboratory laboratories	aluminum
2. customer	experiment
3. contaminate contaminating	unavoidable unavoidably
4. astronauts	resistant
5. advantages	eliminate

Activity J: **Passage Reading and Comprehension**

	"Factories Beyond Earth"
	The sun's intense rays bounced off giant mirrors and were
10	instantly focused on the lump of iron hanging in space. As the
22	temperature of the iron rose, it began to melt. Quickly, two
33	white-suited astronauts floating out of range of the hot rays
44	added a little carbon and aluminum to the molten iron. (#1)
54	"Maybe we should add some nickel from that last asteroid
64	the space miners brought back," one of the astronauts radioed to
75	her co-worker. "We want that steel we're making to be tough and
87	acid-resistant." (#2)
89	"I'll call the customer on my long-range radio and let you
101	know," the other astronaut replied. "Just let the steel hang there
112	in a molten lump until I get an answer."
121	Meanwhile, inside a nearby space factory, a chemist was
130	busy growing crystals for electronic circuits. "I wonder what it was
141	like to grow crystals like these on Earth, where gravity kept them

153	from forming the perfect shape they form here in space," he
164	thought to himself. "I guess chemists had problems in the days
175	when there were no gravity-free laboratories or processing plants.
185	The crystals I'm growing will be used to make the very best
197	computers in the solar system. (#3)
202	Down the hall from the chemist, a biology professor was
212	telling her medical students about the advantages of making
221	medicines in space. "We know from an experiment performed in
231	space way back in 1975 that kidney cells produce much more of a
244	special chemical when they are grown in space than when they
255	are grown on Earth," she explained. "We have recently discovered
265	that, like kidney cells, human pancreas cells will produce more of
276	their special chemical, insulin, when they are grown in space labs.
287	We are also growing bacteria in space that can produce human
298	insulin. Bacteria grow faster in space than on Earth. Growing
308	more human insulin at a faster rate is a big help to people who
322	have diabetes. (#4)
324	"We're also making purer vaccines and medicines here in
333	space than we ever made on Earth," the professor continued. (#5)
343	"Why is that?" asked a student.
349	"Because we don't need to use containers to hold the
359	materials we're mixing," she responded. "Without gravity, they
367	hold together all by themselves. And because we can eliminate
377	containers, we avoid contaminating the materials we're working
385	with. On Earth, microscopic pieces of containers unavoidably got
394	mixed in with the products. There was no such thing as a really
407	pure product on Earth—whether it was a medicine, cosmetic,
417	metal, or glass." (#6)
420	

From *Matter: Building Block of the Universe.* © 1994 by Prentice Hall.
Used by permission.

A.		**Total number of words read**
B.		**Total number of underlined words (mistakes)**
C.		**Total number of words read correctly**

Activity A: **Vowel Combinations Review**

1.	ow	ee	ir	oy	ay	or
2.	au	ou	oo	i - e	oi	o - e
3.	oa	er	ur	ea	ai	ar

Activity B: **Vowel Conversions Review**

i	e	a	o	u

Activity C: **Prefixes and Suffixes Review**

1.	ad	im	be	com	de
2.	con	per	dis	ab	pro
3.	le	al	ity	ence	ly
4.	or	ible	age	ture	ful
5.	ary	able	le	tious	ent

Activity D: **Strategy Practice**

1.	rejection	disrespectful
2.	tenacious	collectively
3.	exaggerate	premeditated
4.	comprehensive	disorganization

Activity E: **Independent Strategy Practice**

1.	complaining	culminate
2.	forgetfulness	establishment
3.	captivate	inconsiderate
4.	commandment	unconventional
5.	impressionable	inspirational

Activity F: **Word Reading Review**

1.	government	instrumentalist
2.	reflective	surrender
3.	exemption	destructive
4.	administrative	contentment
5.	unpredictable	intolerable

Activity G: **Spelling Dictation**

1.	2.
3.	4.

Activity H: **Sentence Reading**

1. The commander was very inconsiderate of the troops.

2. He was not only inconsiderate but also unpredictable and intolerant.

3. His forgetfulness was astonishing.

4. Michael's inventiveness culminated in the design of a new kind of car.

5. Young children are very impressionable and copy everything they see.

6. Terrell's collection of poems is inspirational to all readers.

7. The school's administration was quite unconventional.

8. Because of their forgetfulness and disorganization, we missed the show.

9. The playfulness of the chimp can captivate even indifferent people.

10. Jason is very persistent. His teacher is proud that he is tenacious with his schoolwork, always trying to succeed.

11. Unlawful discrimination can be very destructive.

12. The jury agreed that the murder was premeditated.

Activity I: **Passage Preparation**

Part 1—Tell	
1. climate	biomes
2. ecosystem	lichens
3. taiga	acidic

Part 2—Strategy Practice	
1. organisms	characteristic
2. determine	property
determined	properties
3. temperature	precipitation
4. centimeters	permafrost
5. deciduous	abundant

Activity J: **Passage Reading and Comprehension**

"Land Biomes"

	Would you be surprised to see a polar bear living in a
12	desert? Of course you would. You know that polar bears live in a
25	different kind of area. Scientists have determined that Earth can
35	be divided into eight different areas called biomes. A biome is a
47	large ecosystem with characteristic organisms and nonliving
54	factors throughout. Each biome has certain properties, such as
63	the amount of sunlight, range of temperature, and the amount of
74	precipitation. (#1)
75	The tundra is a land biome with an annual precipitation of
86	nearly twenty centimeters and with mosses and plantlike
94	organisms called lichens. The temperature in the tundra ranges
103	from -60°C in the winter to 15°C in the summer.
113	Most precipitation in the tundra is in the form of snow, and
125	most of the ground is also frozen. During the short summer, the
137	soil thaws through just the top few centimeters. Deeper than that
148	is the permafrost, a layer of soil that is frozen all year. Because of
162	the permafrost, no plants with deep-reaching root systems can
172	grow. Trees can't grow in the tundra. (#2)

179	The taiga (TI guh) is a land biome with an annual
188	precipitation of nearly fifty centimeters. Conifers are the
196	characteristic plants. They are the main kind of tree. The
206	temperature in the taiga ranges from -35°C in the winter to 20°C
218	in the summer.
221	Much of the precipitation is in the form of rain. There is also
234	a lot of fog. Because the temperature is above 0°C for a longer
247	period of time in the taiga than it is in the tundra, the soil thaws
262	completely each year. The soil, though, is very wet and acidic. The
274	acid condition is caused by peat mosses and conifers that grow in
286	the taiga. (#3)
288	The temperate forest is a land biome with an annual
298	precipitation of one hundred centimeters. Deciduous trees are the
307	characteristic plants. The temperature in the temperate forest
315	ranges from -30°C in the winter to 40°C in the summer. The
327	temperate forest biome has four distinct seasons each year:
336	spring, summer, autumn, and winter. (#4)
341	The tropical rain forest is a land biome with an annual
352	precipitation of nearly two hundred to four hundred centimeters
361	of rainfall. Vines and broadleaf trees are the characteristic plants.
371	The temperature in the tropical rain forest is nearly the same all
383	year, around 25°C. Rainfall is abundant all year in a tropical rain
395	forest.
396	The growing season lasts all year long in the tropical rain
407	forest. Plants grow very well in the warm, wet climate. More kinds
419	of plants grow in this biome than in any other. (#5)
429	

From *Science in Your World.* © 1991 by Macmillan/McGraw Hill School Publishing Company.
Reprinted by permission.

A.	☐	**Total number of words read**
B.	☐	**Total number of underlined words (mistakes)**
C.	☐	**Total number of words read correctly**

Activity A: Vowel Combinations Review

1.	oo	er	ou	ur	ow	or
2.	au	ai	ea	oy	au	a - e
3.	ee	oa	ar	e - e	oi	ir

Activity B: Vowel Conversions Review

o	i	u	a	e

Activity C: Prefixes and Suffixes Review

1.	ad	com	a	in	be
2.	pre	pro	ab	im	un
3.	ic	tion	ist	ent	le
4.	ful	sive	ary	cial	ture
5.	est	er	ity	able	tious

Activity D: **Strategy Practice**

1.	estimation	punishable
2.	occupation	meaningfulness
3.	incorruptible	misinformation
4.	individuality	accomplishment

Activity E: **Independent Strategy Practice**

1.	inference	masterfully
2.	circumstantial	murderous
3.	evaluate	environmentally
4.	impracticality	excommunicate
5.	proportionate	departmental

Activity F: **Word Reading Review**

1.	comprehensive	fundamentally
2.	disorganization	premeditated
3.	inconsiderate	communication
4.	inspirational	tentatively
5.	unconventional	investigation

Activity G: **Spelling Dictation**

1.	2.
3.	4.

Activity H: **Sentence Reading**

1. It is a great accomplishment to masterfully read longer words.

2. It is inconsiderate to interrupt a conversation.

3. Misinformation should not be part of good communication.

4. Organization, not disorganization, is needed in most occupations.

5. As you read, you constantly make inferences and evaluations.

6. The scientist will communicate the results of the investigation.

7. The comprehensive test evaluated students' reading and math skills.

8. The corporate department determines if the building plans are environmentally safe.

9. A person is excommunicated when the church removes him or her from the rolls.

10. Music can be meaningful as well as inspirational.

11. Marlene tentatively estimated the room's area as eight square feet.

12. The boss asked each person who worked for her to maintain his or her individuality.

Activity I: **Passage Preparation**

Part 1—Tell		
1.	typhoid	frontier
2.	journeyed	westward
3.	cholera	European

Part 2—Strategy Practice		
1.	tornado	century centuries
2.	settlement	expedition
3.	possessions	territory
4.	romanticize romanticized	resident residency
5.	homesteaders	terrestrial
6.	navigators	accessible

Activity J: **Passage Reading and Comprehension**

"Pioneer Life"

12 | The sky turned red and clouds of dust began to sweep across
21 | the prairie. From inside the tiny Kansas schoolhouse, India
31 | Harris Simmons and her frightened students watched as a black,
40 | funnel-shaped cloud moved straight toward them. They were
53 | miles away from the nearest house, in one of the first schools on
56 | the Kansas frontier.
66 | Suddenly a child standing in the doorway, his face drained
77 | of color, cried out, "It's done turned, teacher. It's going straight
84 | north." The tornado had shifted its course. (#1)
93 | The children opened their books and returned to work.
104 | Having journeyed with their families into a vast new land where
113 | schools, papers, and books were scarce, they desperately wanted
 | to learn. (#2)

115	In the early 1840s, restless young people, many of them
125	farmers with families, saw westward settlement as an adventure.
134	They wanted to escape heavy taxes, and sometimes debts, for a
145	new life away from what they thought of as the crowds back East.
158	But settling the frontier presented serious hardships for men
167	and women alike. Not everyone undertook the dangerous and
176	demanding expedition with enthusiasm. Women left behind,
183	usually forever, relatives, neighbors, and most of their
191	possessions, to be near their husbands and keep their young
201	families together. (#3)
203	Since the Plains Indians did not build upon the land they
214	had inhabited for centuries, European Americans considered
221	Indian territory to be free land. Plains Indians roamed over a
232	wide area searching for buffalo and carrying most of their
242	possessions with them. The early pioneers were often frightened
251	by the Indians and traveled in large groups for protection. But
262	most Indians, while resentful, were curious about the intruders.
271	They readily exchanged salmon and buffalo meat for blankets,
280	cash, and clothing. (#4)
283	In later years, Congress passed laws that enabled
291	homesteaders to claim frontier property if they established
299	residency and made improvements on the land. Gradually, white
308	settlers took most of the Indian lands. (#5)
315	Guidebooks and early settlers' accounts romanticized (gave
322	an appealing quality to) the Pacific Coast. One man who traveled
333	to the Oregon Territory in 1834 described it as a "terrestrial
344	paradise." But the journey was difficult. Women hiked up steep
354	mountains, sometimes carrying small children in their arms,
362	while men hoisted the covered wagons up rocky cliffs with ropes
373	and pulleys. Together they crossed arid deserts and traversed
382	rolling streams in canoes with the help of Indian navigators.
392	Women nursed children and husbands through illness after
400	illness.
401	Clean water was not always accessible and diseases spread
410	rapidly. Cholera and typhoid, carried across the continent by
419	emigrants (people who leave one country to settle in another),
429	proved to be the most deadly illnesses. (#6)
436	

A.		**Total number of words read**
B.		**Total number of underlined words (mistakes)**
C.		**Total number of words read correctly**

Lesson 20

Activity A: **Vowel Combinations Review**

1.	a - e	ow	oi	ay	ee	au
2.	ar	o - e	oo	i - e	or	ea
3.	ai	oy	u - e	ou	i - e	oa

Activity B: **Vowel Conversions Review**

e	o	i	a	u

Activity C: **Prefixes and Suffixes Review**

1.	re	ab	con	im	de
2.	pro	per	dis	com	ad
3.	le	ence	tial	ance	ism
4.	al	ism	le	ary	ly
5.	cious	able	ible	ic	ate

Activity D: **Strategy Practice**

1.	invitation	optical
2.	pardonable	perseverance
3.	unpredictable	deliberation
4.	trepidatiously	repercussion

Activity E: **Independent Strategy Practice**

1.	population	sarcastic
2.	spectator	inconspicuous
3.	incompetent	dissimilarity
4.	contaminate	examination
5.	impressionistic	insurmountable

Activity F: **Word Reading Review**

1.	administrative	dissatisfaction
2.	impracticality	environmentally
3.	tentatively	unpredictable
4.	consistence	communication
5.	government	impressionable

Activity G: **Spelling Dictation**

1.	2.
3.	4.

Activity H: **Sentence Reading**

1. As an attempt to reduce the size of the federal government, administrative departments will be consolidated.

2. He did not find his companion's sarcastic comments entertaining.

3. The written communication contained a number of misconceptions, and was, therefore, confusing.

4. The children watched the evening performance hiding behind curtains, trying to be inconspicuous.

5. Consistency and professionalism are qualities needed in all occupations.

6. The defendant could not submit the circumstantial evidence from the investigation.

7. All corporations thrive on effective organization and environmentally-safe conditions.

8. Historically, our population has always been environmentally concerned.

9. I think the estimate of the number of spectators was exaggerated.

10. Most impressionable children do not act independently.

11. The instrumentalist's recordings were truly inspirational.

12. While the instructor's methods were unconventional, the results were tremendous.

Activity I: **Passage Preparation**

Part 1—Tell

1.	symphonies	South Korea
2.	Huang He River	Tigris River
3.	Euphrates River	society

Part 2—Strategy Practice

1.	Arabic	classical
2.	ancestors	agriculture
3.	irrigate irrigating	civilizations
4.	culture cultural	diffusion
5.	geographers	authoritarian
6.	democracy	constitution

Activity J: **Passage Reading and Comprehension**

"What is Culture?"

	If you wake up to rock music, put on denim jeans, drink
12	orange juice for breakfast, and speak English, those things are
22	part of your culture. If you eat flat bread for breakfast, speak
34	Arabic, and wear a long cotton robe to protect you from the hot
47	sun, those things are part of your culture. (#1)
55	When some people hear the word culture, they think of
65	priceless paintings and classical symphonies. Culture, as used in
74	geography, is the way of life of a group of people who share
87	similar beliefs and customs. These people may speak the same

---

97	language, follow the same religion, and dress in a certain way.
108	The culture of a people also includes their government, their
118	music and literature, and the ways they make a living. (#2)
128	A colorfully dressed dancer in South Korea reflects certain
137	customs that are important to her. Many of her beliefs and
148	customs have been passed down from distant ancestors. All of us
159	hold certain beliefs and act certain ways because of what we've
170	learned in our culture. What things are important in your
180	culture? (#3)
181	Some 4,000 to 5,000 years ago, at least four cultures arose
192	in Asia and Africa. One developed in China along a river called
204	the Huang He. Another developed near the Indus River in South
215	Asia, a third between the Tigris and Euphrates rivers in
225	Southwest Asia, and a fourth along the Nile River in North
236	Africa.
237	All four river-valley cultures developed agriculture and
245	ways of irrigating or bringing water to the land. Why was irrigation
257	important? Farming produced more food than hunting and
265	gathering, which meant that larger populations could develop.
273	People then learned trades, built cities, and made laws. (#4)
282	The river-valley cultures eventually became civilizations,
289	which are highly developed cultures. These civilizations spread
297	their knowledge and skills from one area to another, a process
308	known as cultural diffusion. (#5)
312	The kind of government, or political system, a society has
322	reflects its culture. Until a few hundred years ago, most countries
333	had authoritarian systems in which one person ruled with
342	unlimited power.
344	When the people of a country hold the powers of
354	government, we think of that government as a democracy.
363	Citizens choose their leaders by voting. Once in power, leaders in
374	a democracy are expected to obey a constitution or other long-
385	standing traditions that require them to respect individual
393	freedoms. (#6)
394	Language is a powerful tool, offering a way for people to
405	share information. Sharing a language is one of the strongest
415	unifying forces for a culture. Languages spoken in a culture region
425	often belong to the same language family, or group of languages
436	having similar beginnings. Romance languages, for example, come
443	from Latin, the language of ancient Rome. Spanish, Portuguese,
452	French, Italian, and Romanian are in the Romance language
461	family. (#7)
464	

From *Geography: The World and Its People.*
© 1998 by McGraw-Hill Companies. Reprinted by permission.

A. ☐ Total number of words read

B. ☐ Total number of underlined words (mistakes)

C. ☐ Total number of words read correctly

Strategies
for Reading Long Words

Overt Strategy

1. Circle the prefixes.

2. Circle the suffixes.

3. Underline the vowels.

4. Say the parts of the word.

5. Say the whole word.

6. Make it a real word.

EXAMPLE

reconstruction

Covert Strategy

1. Look for prefixes, suffixes, and vowels.

2. Say the parts of the word.

3. Say the whole word.

4. Make it a real word.

Prefixes, Suffixes, and Vowel Combinations

Decoding Element	Key Word	Decoding Element	Key Word	Decoding Element	Key Word
a	above	**de**	depart	**mis**	mistaken
ab	abdomen	**dis**	discover	**per**	permit
ad	advertise	**en**	entail	**pre**	prevent
be	belong	**ex**	example	**pro**	protect
com	compare	**im**	immediate	**re**	return
con	continue	**in**	insert	**un**	uncover
able	disposable	**est**	biggest	**ment**	argument
age	courage	**ful**	careful	**ness**	kindness
al	final	**ible**	reversible	**or**	tailor
ance	disturbance	**ic**	frantic	**ous**	nervous
ant	dormant	**ing**	running	**s**	birds
ary	military	**ion**	million	**sion**	mission
ate	regulate	**ish**	selfish	**sive**	expensive
cial	special	**ism**	realism	**tial**	partial
cious	precious	**ist**	artist	**tion**	action
ed	landed	**ity**	oddity	**tious**	cautious
ence	essence	**le**	cradle	**tive**	attentive
ent	consistent	**less**	useless	**ture**	picture
er	farmer	**ly**	safely	**y**	industry
ai	rain	**oo**	moon, book	**or**	torn
au	sauce	**ou**	loud	**ur**	turn
ay	say	**ow**	low, down	**a—e**	make
ea	meat, thread	**oy**	boy	**e—e**	Pete
ee	deep	**ar**	farm	**i—e**	side
oa	foam	**er**	her	**o—e**	hope
oi	void	**ir**	bird	**u—e**	use

Row labels (left margin): **Prefixes**, **Suffixes**, **Vowel Combinations**

REWARDS Chart

Name _____

Lesson	First Page Activities A, B, C, D	Second Page Activities E, F, and G	Third Page Activities H, I, and J	Reading Check Activity G	Bonus Points	Total Points	Lesson Grade
Lesson 1							
Lesson 2							
Lesson 3							
Lesson 4							
Lesson 5							
Lesson 6							
Lesson 7							
Lesson 8							
Lesson 9							
Lesson 10							
Lesson 11							
Lesson 12							
Lesson	**Initial Activities**	**Sentence Reading**	**Passage Reading**	**Reading Check**	**Bonus Points**	**Total Points**	**Lesson Grade**
Lesson 13							
Lesson 14							
Lesson 15							
Lesson 16							
Lesson 17							
Lesson 18							
Lesson 19							
Lesson 20							
						Total Points	Overall Grade

Participation Points
- Following behavioral guidelines
- Paying attention and participating
- Responding accurately

Reading Check (line or sentence)
1. Two errors
2. One error
3. No errors

Student Name: _____

Fluency Graph

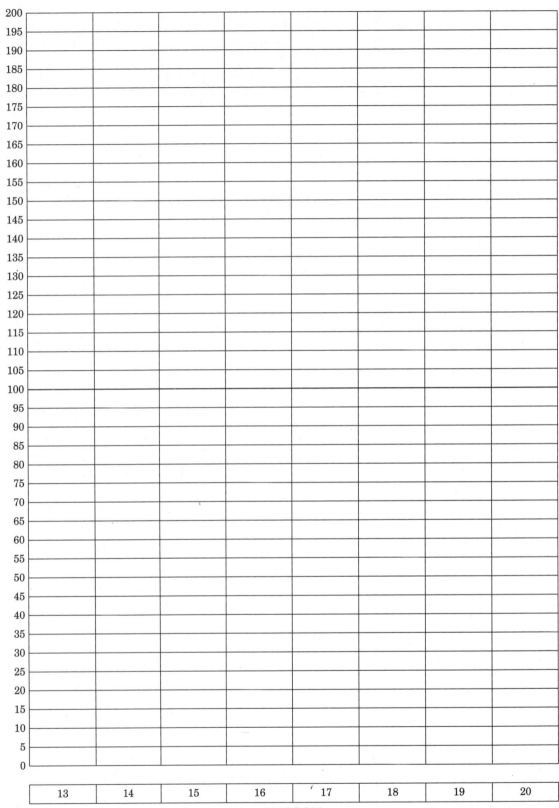

Number of Words Read Correctly Per Minute

| | 13 | 14 | 15 | 16 | 17 | 18 | 19 | 20 |

LESSON

REWARDS Student Book